This book is dedicat children, who have unconditionally and taught us how to do the same.

ISBN-13: 978-1490413587

ISBN-10: 1490413588

We would like to give a special thank you to Dr. Laura Markham, Genevieve Simperingham, and Attachment Parenting International for permission to use your amazing wisdom.

About the Authors

Rebecca Eanes is the founder of www.positive-parents.org and independent researcher of attachment and child development. She has also written *The Newbie's Guide to Positive Parenting*. She is a blessed mother of two and married for 11 years now to her high school sweetheart and best friend for the past 17 years.

Laura Ling is an administrator on the Facebook page Positive Parenting: Toddlers and Beyond and mother of one. Her quest for positive parenting began when traditional advice began to feel too harsh and unsupportive. Although not a parenting expert, Laura researches child development, brain science, and emotional well-being in her 'spare time' and hopes to share what she's learned for the betterment of society.

We do not claim to be a parenting experts, but child advocates, believing that all humans, including children, have the right to be treated with respect and compassion. All opinions expressed in this book are our own and derive from years of research and parenting.

Information contained in this book should not be construed as professional or medical advice.

CONTENTS

PART ONE – POSITIVE PARENTING IN THEORY

PART TWO – POSITIVE PARENTING IN ACTION

Part One – Positive Parenting in Theory

INTRODUCTION

Every parent works toward the same goal – to raise confident, caring, and successful human beings. We want them to be compassionate and kind, to have good morals and self-esteem, to have the ability to stand strong in the face of peer pressure, to make good choices, to be well-behaved and well-mannered, and most of all, we want them to be happy.

Positive parenting empowers our children to reach these goals through a solid foundation of a trusting relationship. We harness the powers of connection, empathetic limits, and positive example to guide our children onto the right paths. Rather than viewing our children as *beneath us* and people we must *control*, we create a bond of mutual respect, working alongside our children to teach them how to control themselves.

Positive parenting isn't a method, but a philosophy – a way of seeing children and our relationships with them. I invite you to strip away the layers of "knowledge" forced upon you by family, media, and culture about how children should be raised. There are lots of studies by brilliant scientists that back up what we do as positive parents –form healthy attachments, lead with empathy, take child development into account –and it's nice to feel validated in our choices by the latest research, but what we're truly doing is going back to our heart - our humanity - to bring up our children in love, not fear.

There is an abundance of resources available which tell parents why traditional parenting practices are not optimal, but few help parents learn what to do in place of traditional practices. In this book, we'll discuss the principles of positive parenting, and then we will go through many scenarios to show you what it looks like when these principles are put into action. Of course, each scenario we will cover could go many different ways, and you'll need to take into account your child's temperament and cues. The purpose of these scenarios is to serve as a guideline, an example of positive parenting in action. The wording used is for the most part deliberate, but in-depth analysis is beyond the scope of this book. Children will spot inauthenticity, so it is much more important that you are genuine than it is for you to follow a specific script. However, it's often helpful to have some sort of example when first starting out. Eventually, you will end up with your own natural way of speaking.

If you're new to this philosophy, it may be helpful to get _The Newbie's Guide to Positive Parenting_ by Rebecca Eanes, which is a beginner's guide that explains what positive parenting is, how it differs from permissive parenting, discusses changing your mindset, gives you tools you can use, breaks down the difference between punishment and limit enforcement, and much more.

Parenthood is a beautiful journey. We don't have to become adversaries with our children; doing so is very unnatural to our humanity. We are all wired for connection, for closeness, and for love. Positive parenting frees us to move from the traditional parenting roles which create friction and rebellion and allows us instead to move into a more natural role which creates cooperation and peace. The inevitable conflicts that arise in a relationship no longer define the relationship, but serve as stepping stones to greater understanding and connection.

NON-PUNITIVE PARENTING PARADIGM SHIFT

The first step in successful positive parenting is changing your mindset. The way we were raised and our experiences throughout life have wired our brains to certain beliefs and habits. We perform them often at an unconscious level, carrying on the actions and tone of our parents, whether good or bad. However, because so many of us were raised with punishment, the *shift in our thinking* is the hardest but most important step in embracing positive parenting.

Everyone will have different experiences, expectations, and values. People will be at different points of their journeys and have different destinations they are comfortable with. Whatever your personal goal, you will likely have to make a change in the way you view children, parents, discipline, punishment, or developmental stages in order to be effective with positive parenting. Western culture maintains that children should "be seen and not heard" and that they require constant supervision to prevent negative behavior. One of the worst insults you can give parents in Western culture is that their child is spoiled and out of control.

There is a false dichotomy that seems to arise from this - either you are strict (and therefore have 'good' children) or you are permissive (and are raising brats who will fill the prisons of tomorrow). Dr. Laura Markham of AhaParenting.com offers a third option, the sweet spot[1] of the authoritative style. (There is a fourth style, uninvolved, but those parents won't be reading this.)

Strict parents have very high standards but aren't very responsive to their child's needs. Much of their parenting energy is spent trying to "keep him in line" through punishment, and power struggles are prevalent.

Permissive parents are very responsive, but do not set limits effectively. Either they can't stand to see their child disappointed or they are rejecting their own strict upbringing. Parental resentment is typically high.

Many parents flip-flop between the two, finding neither totally comfortable nor effective. They will start off permissive, then "lay down the law" when things get out of hand, then slide back into permissiveness when they start feeling more like drill sergeants than parents.

Positive parenting looks for that sweet spot of high expectations and high responsiveness. This authoritative style (unfortunately easily confused with authoritarian, the strict style) provides lots of emotional support along with age-appropriate expectations. The child is given autonomy (self-rule and self-determination) within the framework provided by the parents.

What makes authoritative parenting effective is the connection between the child and the parent. Children want to please us when their feelings are in balance and they feel we're on their side. Punishments erode that connection. It takes a huge leap of faith, though, to do away with punishments for their behavior. How do they learn to behave? Won't they just do it again if they get away with it once? What if the behavior is *really* bad?

No one can guarantee how your children will turn out. They are people in their own right. They will make mistakes along the way. They will do things you don't agree with. No two people will always agree on everything, and *that's OK.* Your children will pick up the values you model for them. Positive parenting isn't going to eliminate all unwanted behaviors or turn your children into something they're not. What it will do is foster a calmer, more loving, and more responsive atmosphere.

The paradigm we hope you come to is one where children are loved and respected as individuals in their own right and not controlled by fear (of punishments, disapproval, or withdrawal of love); one where behaviors are seen as strategies for meeting needs; one where limits are set with empathy; one where all emotions are allowed, but not all behaviors; one where love is unconditional.

POSITIVE PARENTING PRINCIPLES

There are 5 principles from which positive parenting actions derive from.

1. Attachment. As humans, we are wired for connection. Attachment is an ongoing relationship between a parent and child that begins in infancy and continues throughout the child's developmental stages. Having a trusted caregiver who consistently provides care, affection, and support to the child in infancy and early childhood is important for a child to reach his or her full potential.

2. Respect. All humans deserve to be treated in a way that respects who they are as individuals. Respecting our children means we treat their minds and bodies with care, we consistently

meet their needs, and we show them the same respect we want shown to us.

3. Proactive parenting. Being proactive means being aware of your children's behavior and addressing a potential issue at the earliest warning signs, before it turns into a problem. Proactive parenting also means being aware of your child's needs and meeting those needs before a problem behavior arises.

4. Empathetic leadership. Not to be confused with permissive parenting, positive parents do create and enforce limits. We are still in a leadership role. The difference is that we do not set and enforce them with a heavy hand, which often leads to resistance and rebellion, but with empathy and kindness. When our limit is set with

kindness and enforced empathically, our children are more accepting of our rules.

5. Disciplining without punishing. Punishment is distinct from discipline. Punishment simply teaches children that, if they break the rules, they will suffer negative consequences and is only effective in so far that it provokes fear in children. Discipline, however, is teaching children why a specific behavior is wrong, giving appropriate alternatives, and teaching them how to manage and better themselves.

THE DEVELOPING SELF-CONCEPT

One of the most important aspects of a child's development is the formation of her self-concept, or identity – namely, her sense of who she is and what her relation is to other people. Because humans behave according to their self-concept[2], it is critical that you help your child develop a healthy, positive self-concept.

Young children come to see themselves through the eyes of their parents. The way you speak to her is the way she speaks to herself, and her self-talk is what forms her beliefs about herself which are the pillars that hold her self-concept. The most dangerous thing about having a distorted self-concept is that the subconscious mind always works to prove the self-concept true; therefore, if your child has a negative self-concept, believing she is naughty, clumsy, selfish, etc., she will behave in a way which lives up to this self-concept. Also known as the self-fulfilling prophecy, children will internalize the labels placed on them and will live up to what you expect them to be. Therefore, be especially careful of the words you use to describe your child and the labels you place on her. Avoid terms such as naughty, mean, selfish, clumsy, stubborn, and other negative labels. Even seemingly positive labels, such as talented, the best, and gifted put a lot of pressure on children to feel they *have* to live up to enormous expectations, which can sometimes backfire and cause them to react against the label and stop trying to achieve in that area for fear of failing. When a child labeled 'smart' is unable to do something, rather than trying harder, she usually gives up with the assumption that she is not 'smart' at that thing and therefore incapable.

Rather than pin labels on your child, it is best to describe things rather than qualifying them. For example, if your child is a good artist, you might say, "You used a lot of colors and many details." Allow her the freedom to draw her own conclusion that she is proud of her work and a talented artist. Saying to her, "Wow! Look at that! You are the best artist I know!" may turn her off from drawing if she doesn't like the pressure of having to keep up the label, or if she doesn't agree with your assessment.

I'm not implying that you should never praise or celebrate your child's achievements. Of course you should! If you love what she's done, tell her so. If you're proud of her, definitely let her know, just be aware of overly exaggerating the praise. Likewise, when your child does something such as hitting her sister, describe the event without calling her naughty or aggressive. "You just hit your sister. Hitting hurts and I won't allow you to hit" rather than "you naughty girl! How could you be so violent toward your sister?" Young children are not aware that a person can have opposing characteristics. For example, they don't yet recognize that a person can be both good and bad, and so they will internalize *bad* if they hear it often enough, and then of course, you will have trouble as she will subconsciously be trying to live up to that 'bad' self-concept.

The way you treat your children becomes the way they treat themselves. If you are often hard on them, they will learn to be hard on themselves. By the same token, the way you speak to them becomes their self-talk, so be mindful to give them a loving and compassionate inner voice.

BUILDING ATTACHMENT IN INFANCY

Positive parenting begins at birth. I believe positive parenting is a natural extension of attachment parenting; thus we recommend practicing the principles of attachment parenting with infants. Attachment parenting fosters trust, communication, and bonding which will facilitate discipline as the infant grows into toddlerhood. For the best and most thorough explanation of attachment parenting, I look to Attachment Parenting International. The mission of Attachment Parenting International (API) is to promote parenting practices that create strong, healthy emotional bonds between children and their parents. API believes that Attachment Parenting (AP) practices fulfill a child's need for trust, empathy, and affection and will provide a foundation for a lifetime of healthy relationships.

Read more about API at

www.attachmentparenting.org.

Please note that these are API's 8 principles of parenting.

1. <u>Prepare for pregnancy, birth, and parenting.</u> Reflect on childhood experiences and current beliefs about parenting. Become informed on human development within the womb. Work through negative emotions surrounding the pregnancy. Explore different types of birthing options and parenting philosophies. Educate yourself about breastfeeding. Research all aspects of routine newborn care. Educate yourself about developmental stages.

2. <u>Feed with love and respect.</u> Breastfeeding meets the emotional and nutritional needs best;

however, "bottle nursing" is another option.
Feed on cue, before the stage of crying. Maintain
eye contact; talk softly and lovingly. Introduce
solids on signs of readiness, not age. Avoid the
use of food as reward or punishment. Gentle
weaning.

3. Respond with sensitivity. You begin to build
the foundation of trust and empathy by
responding appropriately to your infant's needs.
They learn to trust when their needs are
consistently responded to with sensitivity.
Frequent holding and interactions promote
bonding and secure attachment. Tantrums
represent strong emotions and should be taken
seriously. A parent's role in tantrums is to
comfort the child, not punish. Continue to
nurture a close connection with older children by

respecting the child's feelings and trying to understand the needs behind his behavior.

4. Use nurturing touch. **Nurturing touch stimulates growth-promoting hormones, improves intellectual motor development, and helps regulate baby's temperature, heart rate, and sleep patterns. Cultures high in physical affection, touch, holding, or carrying rate are low in adult physical violence. Skin-to-skin contact is especially effective. Frequent hugs, back rubs, or massage all meet the need for nurturing touch in older children.**

5. Ensure safe sleep, physically and emotionally. Attachment parenting encourages parents to respond to their children through the night just as they do through the day. Parents are encouraged to explore the variety of different

sleeping arrangements and choose the approach that best allows them to be responsive at night. Co-sleeping refers to sleeping in close proximity, often with the child on another sleep surface in the parent's room. Bed sharing describes an arrangement where all family members share the same sleep surface. Bed sharing is recommended only for breastfeeding families. <u>See API's Safe Co-sleeping Guidelines.</u>[3] Routines often help establish healthier sleep habits. Young children who have their own bed often go to sleep more willingly if the parent lies down with them until they are very drowsy or asleep. Children outgrow this need when they are developmentally ready and will happily go to sleep on their own. When the time comes to move the child to his own bed, do the transition gently.

6. <u>Provide consistent and loving care.</u> By
providing consistent and loving care from early
infancy, parents strengthen their relationship
with their child and build a healthy attachment. If
neither parent can be a full-time caregiver, then
the child needs someone who is not only
consistent and loving but has formed a bond with
him. Respect the child's needs and follow his
cues about his readiness to separate. Avoid using
threats, shame, fear, or intimidation to force
separation. It is very important to spend focused
time on reconnecting with the child after a
separation.

7. <u>Practice positive discipline.</u> Positive discipline
begins at birth. The bonds of attachment and
trust formed in early infancy become the
foundation of discipline. Children learn by
example, so it is important to model positive

actions and relationships. Resolve problems in a way that leaves everyone's dignity intact. When parents react in a way that creates tension, anger, or hurt feelings, they can repair any damage to the parent-child relationship by taking time to reconnect.

8. <u>Strive for balance in personal and family life.</u> Striving for balance ensures that everyone's needs – not just the child's – are recognized, validated, and met to the greatest extent possible. The child's needs must be a priority, and the younger the child, the more intense and immediate his needs. Even so, she is one piece of the complete family picture that also includes the needs of the parents, siblings, plus family as a whole.

For a more in-depth definition of each principle and for more information, visit the API Website at www.attachmentparenting.org.[4]

If your child is past the infancy stage and you did not follow the principles of attachment parenting, don't despair. Just because you did not follow all of the attachment parenting principles doesn't mean you "did it wrong" or have damaged your child in any way. It is likely that you were attentive enough to form a good attachment, and there is time now for strengthening your parent-child bond and healing any wounds/trauma.

If you, by the advice of an "expert" or physician, allowed your child to cry-it-out, fed on a schedule, or have already used punishment (either physical or otherwise), forgive yourself. Do not carry around guilt for past mistakes. Look forward to all the time left to connect, and turn your attention toward making the best future you can for your family.

Part Two – Positive Parenting in Action

EXPLORATION/DANGER

Toddlers are biologically programmed to **PLAY** and to **EXPLORE**.[5] Both are crucial in toddlerhood. Don't squelch your little one's curiosity, but instead provide a safe place for her to explore and begin *teaching* her what is off-limits through language, play, and empathetic limit-setting.

Don't mistake independence for defiance. Some toddlers are more strong-willed and independent than others.

Develop a habit of seeing through your toddler's eyes. From your perspective, you're using your stern voice and redirecting him when he goes for the outlet. From his perspective, he's learning cause and effect. "Every time I go near this thing, mommy changes her voice, jumps up, and scoops me away! How fun!" So, his smile as he heads toward the outlet again isn't defiance; it's a game.

Save your "danger voice" for the biggies. The average toddler hears the word "no" an astonishing 400 times a day, according to experts. If you use a big voice or yell out often, or use "no" a lot, this will soon lose effect. Your child may not be able to tell the difference between "NO! Stove hot!" and "NO! No cookie!" All she hears is "NO!" and if she hears it often, *it doesn't signal danger*. Consider using alternatives to "no" and use different words for actual danger, such as "DANGER!" or "STOP!" which are more likely to catch your child's attention. If you find those words losing effectiveness, try counting how many times you are saying them in a day.

Scenario #1:

Your 18 month old is a little explorer. She really likes to climb, too! She can even climb up in the chair, then up on the kitchen table.

Behind the behavior: Age appropriate developmental growth. Remember her strong drive to *play* and *discover*. If she's wanting to climb (or run, or throw, or jump), she is just wanting to *play*. Children have a need for certain types of activities, some of which may make their parents' hearts stop. A young toddler doesn't understand why you don't want her to "discover" climbing on the table, although she will typically self-regulate and not attempt anything she is certain she cannot do. Part of the process is discovering what she can and cannot do, and it does require crossing that line a few times.

Younger toddlers can be redirected and older toddlers can be shown potential dangers and directed to an alternate way of meeting the need to climb, run, throw, or jump.

ACTION: The first time your child attempts to climb on the table, you intervene, saying, "Climbing is fun! Let's find a safe place for you to climb. This table is not safe and you might get hurt if you fall." Let her climb over some couch cushions, if she wants. Climbing itself is not misbehavior. She may conquer Mount Everest one day! The goal is to keep her safe and teach her what is appropriate. If you overstate the risk, or make it a given ("You will fall and bust your head open!"), over time, your child will stop believing you and give your warnings less weight. The next time she heads for the table, immediately and gently take her from the table, repeating the above. If she gets upset, acknowledge her upset. "I see you're mad. You want to climb, but that isn't safe. Let's go play over here." Remember that climbing is fun, so make your replacement activity just as appealing. This is not a bribe; it's an alternative to a behavior that is unacceptable to you.

Scenario #1.1

What if you've repeated the above steps 14 times and she continues to head for the table?

Behind the behavior: Unmet needs. There are two possible explanations for the continued behavior, both based on needs not being met *according to the child.* It's not always clear if a child needs more of something or something else entirely. Mindful observation can help, but don't expect to always be able to tell.

Maybe her need for climbing has not been met yet. She is not deliberately disobeying you because it's fun to watch your face turn red (interesting, perhaps, and maybe something worth exploring more) but because she is acting to get a need met. As frustrating as it can be to repeatedly redirect a child from the same activity, it does not stem from any malicious thought on her part at all.

Children learn from repetition. You will sing the alphabet song hundreds of times. You will repeat warnings ad nausem. The developing brain requires the repetitions to cement the thought and to build patterns, and then, even after the child *knows* an action is not desirable; it will be quite some time before she can control her impulses. The part of the brain that controls planning and restraint doesn't fully mature until the mid-twenties[6]; that's two decades from now, so scale back your expectations accordingly.

Maybe her need for attention has not been met. Children don't yet have appropriate strategies for getting their needs met. They just know something is not right and are trying to restore internal balance. If your child discovers that you will immediately come get her when she climbs, she may use that strategy to get your undivided attention, should she feel that need is not being completely met. (And yes, even though you may spend what seems like every minute of the day with her, engaged with her, *she* still doesn't feel her needs have been met. In this case, you probably do need to try something different, not just more of the same attention.)

ACTION: You may need to plan more climbing activities or find something different to climb. What was fun last month may no longer be a challenge. Perhaps a trip to a playground is in order instead of staying home. Maybe a different location will do the trick.

Take 10 minutes (or more!), dance around the living room, play hide and seek, read her a book, it doesn't matter what you do as long as your attention is fully focused on her. Fill her cup, and she won't need to head for the table again (for a while).

Another option is to put up a baby gate.

Modifying the environment limits the negative interactions and is a positive solution that sets your child up for success.

Scenario #2:

Your 2-1/2 year old son doesn't like to hold hands when walking through parking lots or large crowds. Every time you try to hold his hand, he pulls it away and tries to run, or he fusses at you and claims, "I can do it myself!"

Behind the behavior: Independence. It's a toddler's job to start developing his autonomy and that means doing things on his own. Because he's just starting to develop empathy (being able to see things from another's point of view) he doesn't realize that the drivers may not see him or be able to stop in time. He just knows that he wants to walk the way he wants to walk and that running is fun, too.

NOTE: Safety is non-negotiable. I wouldn't say to him, "Well OK, but please stay close" and risk him darting in front of a car or losing him in a crowd. Remember, positive parenting is not permissive parenting. While it's important to foster independence and competency, it's more important to keep him safe.

ACTION: Before getting out of the car, explain to your toddler what is going to happen. If you can offer him a choice, do so. "Would you like to ride in the stroller or hold my hand?" If the stroller/cart is not an option, explain in simple terms that you must keep him safe, and to do that, he needs to hold your hand. As you take his hand, try to engage him in something that takes his mind off the hand-holding. "Let's look for red cars" or "let's skip to the door." If he cries or protests, empathize with his upset. Get down on his level. "I know you want to walk by yourself, but my job is to keep you safe. I don't want you to get lost! Now let's look for red cars! There's one! Do you see another?" If he still struggles to free himself, carry him. You may have to endure a few unpleasant ventures. Acknowledge his need and empathize with his upset, but stick to your limit. He'll soon learn it's a non-negotiable.

Scenario #3:

Your 3 year old enjoys cooking with you in the kitchen. He sees you put something in the oven and goes over to open it up and take a look himself.

Behind the behavior: Curiosity. "What did mom

just put in? What does this thing do, anyway?" Not only is he curious, he learns how to fit into this world by imitating you. While it's not always desirable (as anyone who has let profanity slip knows), it's evolutionarily beneficial. We *want* our children to be curious and learn from us, even though it can be frustrating at times.

ACTION: "DANGER!" He stops and looks at you. You smile at him and back him up from the oven. Open it while you are holding him at a safe distance. "See the casserole? The oven is very hot and will bake it so we can eat it! Feel the heat coming from the oven? It can burn you and give you a big ouchie, so don't touch it. Are you ready to help me make dessert?"

Scenario #4:

Your 10 month old crawls over to the dog and

begins sticking her finger in his ear, pulling his whiskers, and chews on his tail. He's a great dog, but what if he bites her? And what about all the germs?

Behind the behavior: Curiosity. Babies recognize humans, and although they're fascinating, too, pets are different and worthy of being checked out. They also respond in interesting new ways and have a variety of textures, smells, and sounds.

ACTION: Safety first - never leave animals and small children alone, no matter how gentle or tame or 'good with children' they are. Accidents happen and you can never predict exactly how another living creature will respond.

If your pet doesn't get agitated when examined,

show your baby how to pet gently by holding her hand and stroking his fur. Explain that certain areas are sensitive and to be extra gentle or avoid touching. Show her the different sensations of soft fur, wet nose, sharp claws, and hot breath. Plan on repeating this exercise many times, but even when she 'gets it', don't leave her alone with him.

If your pet does not appreciate the attention, separate them as much as possible. Even if you are right there with them, the animal may cause permanent damage before you can react. Be prepared to redirect your daughter and explain "Max wants to sit by himself," or "Max is too tired to play with you" so that she knows there is a reason to give this animal space, not that every dog is mean or to be avoided.

Once your baby becomes more mobile, she may be relentless in her pursuit of the family pet. If he has a safe spot or a way to escape, trust that he will use it if he has to. Cats, for some reason, like to hang around giving disdainful looks, making us think the baby is tormenting them. They will leave when they've had enough, though.

Any animal you are not familiar with should not be approached, however, without the owner's permission. If there is any doubt, keep your distance. Children who have traumatic experiences with animals may become terrified of the breed, the species, or animals in general. Practice approaching the owner with, "Hi, is your dog friendly with kids?" and petting the animal in a non-threatening manner. Scratching under the chin is better received than patting on top of the head. Demonstrate gentle touch until you're sure your child won't be rough.

SUMMARY:

Safety is non-negotiable, so you need to act immediately to keep him from getting hurt; however, your intervention shouldn't also hurt. Place yourself between the danger and your child or gently move them to a safer spot. Smacking teaches the child to fear **you,** not the dangerous object you want to protect them from. Besides, you're not going to be there to smack his hand away when he's 16 and someone is offering him a joint. Build a deeply connected, trusting relationship with him now so that he will listen to your warnings of danger when he's older.

HITTING/AGGRESSIVE BEHAVIOR

First, it is important to understand that children who are aggressive are children who are scared, hurt, or feeling disconnected. Small children with limited language and self-awareness lack the sophistication to tell us what is bothering them or maybe even know themselves. Aggression in older children can be a cover-up of those more vulnerable feelings, especially if they have not been taught how to express them appropriately. I would like to also add that children under the age of 6 don't yet have full access to higher brain functions which allow them to pause and reason. When a young child becomes scared or hurt or is feeling disconnected, they go into that *fight or flight mode*[7], operating out of their brain stem, and have little control over their actions. It is for this reason that an aggressive child needs help, not punishment.

Scenario #1:

Your 3 year old has become aggressive toward her baby sister. She tries to hit her and push her over. You're concerned she's really going to hurt the baby.

Behind the behavior: Jealousy, probably. It's hard sharing mom and dad, especially when you used to have them all to yourself. She may fear being 'replaced' by the baby and doesn't understand the demands put on the parents. From her perspective, nothing good has come of this new person entering the house.

ACTION:

1. Set a limit. ("I won't let you hit.")

2. Offer empathy and acceptance of her feelings. ("You are disappointed.")

3. Let her discharge her feelings by crying with your comfort.

4. Help her explore ways to shift her mood.[8]

To expand on this a bit, you will take her safely away from the baby, get down eye-level with her, and set the limit – "I won't let you hit" (or push, or bite). It is important to acknowledge her feelings of anger or frustration or jealousy that caused her to hit. "You're feeling upset at the baby. Are you upset that I was holding her?" or "she grabbed your toy and that made you angry." Your child is hurting, even though she may look like she isn't. She needs to know it's safe to show her feelings. Tell her it's OK to be angry, and it's OK to cry, and that you will keep everyone safe. If she melts down in your arms, she is healing. Let her get her emotions out while you provide comfort. After the incident is over and everyone is calm, address the reason behind the behavior.

1. Spend special one-on-one time with each child. Let her pick the activity. Connect with her. She needs to know that she is still just as loved as before, even if you think she already knows.

2. Teach appropriate ways to handle anger. You can do this by talking it through, modeling it, role-playing, puppet shows, books, or stories.

3. Don't punish her for hitting. At 3, remember she didn't have the cognitive resources to stop and think about her actions logically. Teaching her how to handle her anger will serve her much better than punishing her for handling it wrong.

4. Read books to her about babies and about being a big sister.

Scenario #2:

Your 19 month old is a biter. He has just bitten another child at a play date.

Behind the behavior: It depends on what was happening at the play date. It could be frustration, anger, hurt feelings, or fear. Toddlers, even very verbal ones, know many more words than they can say. When something triggers a primal emotion, they will have access to even fewer words. Because the mouth is central to learning at this age, biting is a common expression of discomfort.

ACTION: Remember the steps above. Remove your child to safety, make sure the child bitten is

OK, and then set or reinforce your limit. "I won't let you bite." Validate his feelings; empathize with his upset. "You got mad because he took your truck. I see you're mad, but it's not OK to bite. Biting hurts." Let your child express his emotion safely, and problem-solve later. The reason I suggest not talking about appropriate alternatives during the time it happens is because children do not take information in well when they are in fight or flight mode or are upset. They are much more likely to learn and retain information when they are calm.

Don't bite him to show him how it feels. You'd be surprised at how many parents would advise you to do this. Remember, you are the model for appropriate behavior!

Scenario #3:

You got a call from school. Your 6 year old son punched another student for calling him a bad name.

Behind the behavior: Anger, obviously, and lack of ability to control his actions.

ACTION: While a 6 year old is getting better at managing his anger, this is sometimes hard for adults to do, so it isn't surprising that a child hasn't mastered this yet. When you pick him up from school, you're going to have to control your own anger. Model! Reserve judgment and ask him what happened. Empathize with his hurt feelings at being called a name. It does hurt! Now, because this is not a toddler, you may be tempted to punish or give him a consequence, but that isn't going to solve the problem or teach him how to handle a situation like this better the next time. It's time to problem-solve. Let him do most of the problem-solving with your guidance as needed. You might ask:

1. How can you fix what you've done because the student you punched is hurt, too? If he doesn't come up with an answer, offer a few alternatives, such as call and apologize or write an apology letter.

2. What can you do the next time you get called a name or there is a confrontation? Let him brainstorm. It's good if he comes up with alternatives on his own. If he draws a blank, help him out. You may suggest he walk away, work it out with words, or get help from an adult if the situation requires it.

SUMMARY:

Aggressive behavior is very common in young children and peaks from ages 2-4[9]. While this is a common phase kids go through, it is our responsibility to set appropriate limits and teach alternatives. Discipline is always about teaching them right, not punishing the wrong. With empathy and loving guidance, your child will learn appropriate ways to handle her emotions, and this phase will become a distant memory.

TANTRUMS

If you have a toddler, chances are you have experienced a tantrum. Tantrums are not bad behavior but rather a child expressing emotions that are too big for her to handle. She isn't trying to be manipulative; she simply doesn't yet know how to handle big feelings. Children don't like having tantrums any more than you like seeing them. Ignoring a child who is having a tantrum sends the message "I'm not there for you when you're upset." Getting angry at the child scares them and sends the message that they're not lovable when expressing some emotions. He may stop *showing* feelings, but he won't stop *feeling* them. Rather, when we calm our children through these emotional storms, they learn better how to calm themselves.

While it's critical to support your child through her tantrum, it's important to not change your position if that is what triggered the outpouring of big feelings. Eventually, this *will* lead to the manipulative tantrums older children throw to get what they want. If there's a doubt as to whether a tantrum is manipulative or not, give her the benefit of the doubt and treat it as a legitimate outpouring of emotion.

Scenario #1:

Your 18 month old is happily stacking blocks. Suddenly, the blocks fall over, and he begins to wail and flail. What happened? He was happy 4 seconds ago.

Behind the behavior: Frustration. Most likely, a lot of little frustrations throughout the day have been building, and the blocks falling were the last straw. Look for what could be causing unnecessary frustration throughout the day. Does he hear "no" 500 times? Is he still mostly non-verbal? Imagine how annoying it must be to not be able to communicate what you're needing or feeling. Is he getting enough rest? Lots of things can cause frustration to build. Look for the causes and address them. However, don't expect to avoid all tantrums as children have a different perspective of what is important, and cues can be misread. As the child becomes more able to express himself, tantrums will decline (if they have not been rewarded).

ACTION: All he needs from you at this point is understanding. He's got big emotions, and he needs to release them. Depending on your child, hold him, rock him, or just stay near. You might say, "You're so frustrated! It's OK. I'm right here."

Wait with him until it passes. If it's a minor upset, you may be able to improve his mood with humor, but if it's major, he needs to get it out. Just love him through it. It will pass, and not only this tantrum, but this entire stage, and it will pass quickly.

Scenario #2:

Your 3 year old wants ice cream for dinner. (Sounds yummy to me, too!) You, however, have dinner on the stove, and you know ice cream doesn't exactly cover the 4 basic food groups. *You might be able to side-step the tantrum with a "Yes! You can have ice cream after dinner" instead of just "no" but, then again, maybe not.* Realizing she is not getting ice cream right now, she has a meltdown.

Behind the behavior: Autonomy or frustration.

At 3, she may want a little more control, and deciding what she wants for dinner seems perfectly reasonable to her. If she has been grappling for independence recently, you can give her control over all the areas you don't need control over. Let her decide her snacks. Let her pick out which plate. Let her match (or mismatch) her own outfits. This will help fill her need for autonomy, and she'll be more likely to cooperate when you need the control.

Or, this could just be another case of frustration. Being 3 isn't always a walk in the park. Look for ways to ease her frustration levels through the day. Do you have too many unnecessary limits? Is she constantly spatting with a sibling? Is there tension in the home? Address the reason behind the frustration, and she won't melt down so much.

ACTION: Empathy will always be your first step in addressing tantrums. She doesn't need the ice cream, but she does need to know that you *get her*. If you send her away for tantruming, it will just build more bad feelings on top of what she already has. It's OK to be upset that you can't get what you want. Be present for her. You might say, "Wow, you're upset. You really want ice cream right now!" Truly empathizing with her upset is likely to reduce tantrum time, but remain present and calm (just breathe!) until she lets it all out. Explaining why she can't have the ice cream mid-tantrum is futile. She's in fight or flight mode (throwing in some brain science here) and it's best to save the lesson for when she's regulated (calm). Later, you can explain why ice cream isn't a good dinner choice, but during the tantrum, she just needs your presence and empathy.

Note If she has aggressive tantrums (i.e. kicks or hits) or tells you to go away, keep at a safe distance, but don't leave. Let her know you accept her, big emotions and all. "I won't leave you alone while you have these big feelings. I'll be right here if you need me." If she comes after you or someone else, block her from hurting anyone with the minimum amount of force possible. "It's OK to be mad. It's not OK to hit." Try to keep your interaction minimal while she is angry, as this may just feed the tantrum.

You may notice a point when she goes from furious to sad and starts to glance over at you. This is when she will become receptive to soothing and will probably come over for snuggles if you appear welcoming. However, it's still a bit too early to talk about what happened. "I still love you, honey. I'm here." After her heartbeat slows and she appears calmer, you can talk about options. "You were angry that I wouldn't let you have ice cream for dinner. It does sound like a yummy dinner, but it's not good for your tummy. It's OK to be upset. It's not OK to hit. Would it help to hit a pillow to get your angry feelings out?"

She may surprise you by remembering it next time and refrain from hitting you.

Scenario #3:

You've taken your 2 year old with you shopping. You've been out for a few hours now, and the crankiness has been increasing over the past hour. She grabs her sippy, but it's empty, so she hurls it to the floor and begins to cry. Hard. You're already noticing the looks from the other shoppers.

Behind the behavior: Hunger? Tiredness? Over-stimulation? Boredom? Many people are sensitive to fluctuating blood sugar levels or tiredness and will become cranky when they try to do more than their body can handle. Fill the need, whether it is food or a nap or a break, once the tantrum has passed, and chalk it up to a learning experience for the next trip.

ACTION: What's the word of the day? EMPATHY! Who cares if everyone is staring? Focus on your baby and maybe the onlookers will learn something. "I know you're so tired! I'm sorry, sweetie. I've kept us out too long today, and you've missed your nap. We're going home just as soon as I check out. Can you wait that long?" Of course, be prepared to leave your cart where it is and go home if the answer is no. If you don't want to do that, just keep reassuring her that you'll be taking care of her very soon. Sometimes it's worth finishing your errand, to pick up medication, for example, and sometimes it's not. Either way, stay with her through the tantrum, empathize with her upset, and remain calm.

And because we usually really do care if people are judging us, focusing completely on her has the benefit of making it more difficult to see those who are judging us. You are responsible for the physical and emotional well-being of your child, not people you will likely never see again. Publicly apologizing to your child for missing lunch or nap time or just staying out too long gives people an out if they were about to judge you for your child having a meltdown as well.

Scenario #4:

Your 6 year old asks you for a new scooter like his friend has. You tell him you can't afford it right now. He yells back at you that he never gets anything he wants, his friend's parents *buy him everything*, and then he goes into full-on fit mode, stomping, slamming doors, and throwing things.

Behind the behavior: At 6, he should probably be past the tantrums, so you might need to do a little detective work. Perhaps there is peer pressure of some kind, or maybe even bullying that you're not aware of. His desire to fit in may be why he wants the scooter, and may be driving the tantrums. Or perhaps he just hasn't learned how to handle his emotions very well yet. It's time to teach him how. How do you teach him? You guessed it!! EMPATHY.

ACTION: It doesn't matter if your child is 1, 6, 15, or 35, when he is upset, he needs understanding and empathy. The lessons can come later, but during the time of extreme upset, he needs you to be the rock. The drill is the same. Let him know that you see he is upset and that you're there for him.

Once the storm has passed and your child is calm, address the behaviors of kicking, hitting, slamming doors, or throwing things. Explain that the *feelings* are acceptable but these *actions* are not because they could cause injury. Talk about better ways of handling anger and frustration with your child; counting to 10, going outside to throw a ball, or for younger children, clapping releases that energy, or perhaps an **optional** cool down spot filled with books or soothing music. Solicit his input, too. He may have an idea for what helps him regain control that you wouldn't have thought of. Punishing him for kicking won't teach him a more appropriate way to handle his frustration, but only add to his bad feelings.

Until we give children better tools to deal with tough emotions, we can't expect them to do better.

SUMMARY:

Permissive parents give in to tantrums by giving the child ice cream or buying the scooter, authoritarian parents may punish the child for having a tantrum, but positive parents stay within their set boundaries while empathizing and helping the child deal with her emotions.

It is also important to realize that being loving and present through a tantrum doesn't teach your child it's OK to have tantrums. Tantrums are a result of built up emotions that need released. Think of a time when you've been extremely upset. Perhaps your spouse or a friend was there with you while you cried or ranted, holding you, squeezing your hand, *listening*. It didn't send the message to you that it's good to be upset and rant, and it didn't cause you to rant more frequently. **When someone is present and comforting through our upsets, it helps us recover faster and makes us feel connected and loved.**

We want to show our children that we accept them all the time, when the waters are calm AND through the raging storms. This is unconditional love.

NOT LISTENING/COOPERATING

Getting young children to listen and cooperate is one of the main concerns we hear from parents. Often, the very tools we use to try to gain cooperation (nagging, lecturing, and demanding) are what cause our children to tune us out. Punishments or threatened punishments may compel a child to act but doesn't gain their cooperation and may create resentment that lessens the chances of real cooperation later. The stronger our connection with our children, the more likely they are to want to cooperate with us. Cooperation is not the same as obeying, and it's important to note that if you want your child to give cooperation freely, they have to have the option to not cooperate. Safety issues are non-negotiable, but keep in mind that forcing compliance erodes your connection, so it's best used sparingly. Other areas can be examined to see if we're insisting on things being our way when they don't really need to be. Perhaps a common goal can be agreed upon but the path there determined by the child. You may have heard the saying "you can tell me what to do or you can tell me how to do it, but not both."

When your child chooses not to cooperate, you should look first at your relationship. **We want to help people when we feel good about them and ourselves.** What can you do to repair the connections? If your relationship seems strong, you should look at what you're requesting. Does your child have a compelling reason to not cooperate? Our agendas are not automatically our children's agendas and they may not see the value in a clean room, or brushed teeth, or seatbelts. If I can't think of a good reason to tell my child why to do something, it's probably a personal preference and not something I should force on my child at the expense of our relationship.

Even highly connected children will not want to cooperate 100% of the time. There are ways to increase chances of cooperation regardless of the level of connection, though. Clearly and concisely state your request, and only phrase it as a question if you will accept "no" as an answer. "It's time to put on your clothes" as opposed to "can you put on your clothes?"

Use a firm and respectful tone at a conversational distance. Barking commands from across the room is less effective than walking over, getting their attention, and then speaking. Being snide or mocking or condescending will almost certainly cause your child to resist, even if he'd otherwise be willing.

Look for clues to their resistance. This is where you model effective listening. After your child speaks, replay what you have understood him to mean. Don't worry; if you get it wrong, he'll correct you. But, if you get it right, you have valuable information, and he may even share more. Use this understanding to negotiate a solution acceptable to both of you.

Be willing to change your mind. It is not a sign of weakness to be convinced by a good argument. Your children will appreciate your flexibility and the practice of negotiating can even help protect them against peer pressure later.

"Give 'em an inch and they'll take a mile' mostly describes the behavior of people who have hitherto been given only inches. " — Alfie Kohn, "Beyond Discipline"[10]

Scenario #1:

Your 2 year old drew a lovely creation on your wall with a marker (washable, thankfully!) and you want to her wash it off. You direct her to do so, but she continues playing and ignores your request.

Behind the behavior: She's 2, and playing is more fun than cleaning. She may not have actually heard you, either. Until around 3 years old, the brain may be in a different conscious state than we're used to as adults. All stimuli are treated roughly equal, and picking out the *important* parts is more difficult. If you've ever been to a new place where you don't speak the language, you're close to what researchers suspect it's like for babies and toddlers. You may miss cues such as street signs and get lost easily. You may not be able to navigate and hold a conversation at the same time.

ACTION: Make sure you have her attention first. Get down on her level and wait for her to acknowledge you. If you did this, then think about how you originally stated your request. Did you use a kind and assertive tone? Did you phrase it as a question? Asking opens up the possibility of a negative response. Did you angrily demand? Children may tune out anger and yelling as a defense mechanism. A kind and assertive request sounds like this. "Uh-oh, marker is for paper, not walls. Get a wash cloth and clean it off, please." At 2, she is likely going to need help with this request. Remember to keep in mind what is age-appropriate in your expectations. Hand her a wash cloth and point to the wall. If she turns away, ask her if she needs help. Show her how to wipe the wall with the cloth and hand it back to her, pointing to it again, and say "Wash it off, please."

Scenario #2:

Your 4 year old starts tugging on you and the baby when you sit down to feed him. You tell her, "It makes it more difficult to feed Bobby when you pull on us and I'm worried he might get hurt," but she keeps pulling and grabbing. In desperation, you yell "stop!" and she does, for a moment, but now everyone is upset and she goes back to tugging on you.

Behind the behavior: Insecurity. When a child demands our attention, she needs it. Negative attention is still attention, and small children are still learning appropriate ways to get their needs met. It saddens me that parents are sometimes given the advice to not reward a child who *just wants attention*. We are social creatures and attention is a valid need, as much as food and sleep.

ACTION: In the moment, you will need to find a way to meet her need for attention. As a preventative measure, give her attention before she asks for it. Think about the difference between a spontaneous hug and "I love you" from someone and one that comes after you express doubts about the relationship. It tends to mean more to us when it doesn't feel prompted.

When your two children have competing needs, one will have to wait. There is no answer that is always right; you'll have to evaluate who has the greater or more urgent need at the time. "Sweetie, I know you need some attention from me right now. Bobby is already so hungry he's crying. I need to feed him and then we can play whatever you want. Would you like to color next to us on the couch while you wait?"

It's tempting to always put the new baby before the older child, who is better able to wait. But your 4 year old is still only 4 years old. "I know you're hungry, Bobby. I'll feed you in just a moment. Hang on for me. Sweetie, I can see you need some attention from me. Would you like a hug? Once I get Bobby settled, we can read a book, if you like."

Later that day, seek out your 4 year old for some reconnecting. Give her your complete focus and let her determine how you spend your time together. If at all possible, let her be the one to end it, otherwise give her fair warning. "While Bobby is sleeping, I'm all yours. I'll have to get him when he wakes up, but we can do whatever you want until then." If that means laundry falls behind or the floors aren't vacuumed or you have sandwiches for dinner (or all three!), that's OK. Your child is more important than a clean house and once the crisis passes, you'll spend less energy proactively giving positive attention than trying to reactively deal with negative attention.

Scenario #3:

Mornings are always a rush, and it seems your 6

year old is always dawdling instead of getting dressed and ready for school.

Behind the behavior: Different agendas. Children don't run on the same time schedules we do. They have different priorities and may not understand why it is important for you to be on time.

He may also still be having difficulty with multiple step instructions, and it's just too much for him to be fully responsible for his morning routine alone.

ACTION: It's time to re-think the morning routine. Set him up for success by ensuring he gets adequate sleep at night and rises early enough in the morning so that you don't have to be in a hurry. It may be helpful to set up a visual morning routine chart so that he can see exactly what needs to be done. Then, instead of nagging, you can just refer him to his chart to see what needs to be done. You can make a chart with Velcro smiley faces or a pocket to place completed cards in so that he feels a sense of accomplishment when a task is complete. You can offer him reminders, such as, "We are leaving in 15 minutes. What is left on your chart to do?" If he is still having trouble completing his tasks, you can discuss it in a family meeting and brainstorm ways to help him be successful. The goal is to put the responsibility of getting ready on him and off of you, and the more say he has in his routine, the more likely he is to comply. However, it's more important that you help him be successful than it is for him to get ready completely on his own. If he is not cognitively ready for the responsibility, no amount of troubleshooting will make it different. There are whole shelves at bookstores devoted to helping adults with time management and organization. You probably know at least one person (maybe it's you) who is always losing his keys. To shame a child for not being able to do things that seem so effortless to others can impact him the rest of his life, so keep trying solutions until you find something that works for you.

SUMMARY:

I have read "positive parenting" books that advise letting your child experience the natural consequence of not getting dressed by taking him to school in his pajamas. For my son, this would be a form of public humiliation as he doesn't even want to wear his pajamas on pajama day. While I believe sometimes it is best to allow your child to experience natural consequences for his actions, I believe you must use discretion. It is better to set your child up for success and then help him succeed.

Listening and cooperation comes through connection, consistency, and capability. Focus on strengthening your relationship so that you are securely connected, be consistent and follow through with your requests, and make sure your child is capable of completing your requests before expecting him to do so. Once the "3 C's" are met, your child is much more likely to listen and cooperate.

WHINING

Whining, even though it is what Dr. Sears calls a smallie[11] behavior, it can still grate on a parent's nerves. Why? Dr. Laura Markham of www.ahaparenting.com[12] tells us: "Because whining is your little one's more mature form of crying. She's letting you know she needs your attention, and human grownups are programmed to react to whining as much as to crying, so the needs of tiny humans get met. So the minute you hear that whine, you react with anxiety. You'll do anything to stop it. But if you can take a deep breath and remind yourself that there's no crisis, you'll feel a lot better, and you'll parent better."

Most positive parenting experts will advise you to simply ignore whining or tell the child you will not respond to a whiny voice. That advice may be appropriate as long as you know the child is only whining to get your attention and not because there is a deeper issue. *Note, however, that you should never ignore the child, just the whining.* Children may whine for all sorts of reasons, and their whining may actually be a cry for connection or help with something, such as pent-up emotions. As always, meet the need behind the behavior if you can discern what that need is, and the problem will resolve. However, if you suspect that your child is just whining because she thinks you'll give in to her requests, there are some things you can do.

1.   Be sure your child is getting lots of positive attention from you without having to seek it. If your child's cup is full, whining is less likely to be an issue.

2. Teach your child the difference between a strong voice and a whiny voice. She may not even be aware she is using a whiny voice. You can do this by role-playing or using puppets or toys to show the differences between the two tones. Tell your child you can understand her better when she uses her strong voice.

3. Some children whine because they feel powerless or unheard. Make sure your lines of communication stay clear and that your child knows she is a valuable part of the family and her needs matter. Give her choices throughout each day to give her some control.

4. Teach your child negotiating skills. This will alleviate the powerlessness that often causes whining and teaches your child a crucial life skill. Teaching her to control her emotions, state her

need/want in a respectful manner, and work to find solutions that will satisfy everyone's needs will serve her well as she grows.

5. Remain empathetic with your child's experience, but don't give in to whining.

Scenario

Your 3 year old wants to go to the playground. You tell him there is no time today for the playground, so he begins to whine about it.

Behind the behavior: He is frustrated, feeling powerless to get what he wants, and doesn't yet have the ability to cope well with these emotions.

ACTION: Offer a hug first, without saying a word about the whining. Hugs are magical; often times the comfort of your loving arms will soothe him and end the whining. Should he be persistent with the whining, empathize with him. "You really want to go to the park today. I understand." Stick to your limit, "I'm sorry, but our schedule is just too full today." However, if you can squeeze in some park time, there is nothing wrong with negotiating, as long as he doesn't use his whiny voice to get his way. You can tell him, "We might be able to squeeze it in, but I don't like your whiny voice. Remember the strong voice we practiced? Let's talk about what we can do to find the time. Will you help me get everything on our shopping list as quickly as possible and get right into your carseat when we're done?"

SUMMARY:

Some parents feel they give up authority if they

negotiate with their children, but this isn't so at all. Negotiations are a part of life, and learning to do it respectfully creates win/win situations. Your child will feel that you respect her and reflect that respect back to you.

INTERRUPTING

Interrupting is another smallie behavior that can feel like a big deal at the time. Children seem to know when you're having an important conversation with someone else, and they want your attention during that time. If your child continually interrupts you, here are a few steps you can take.

Model! Be mindful not to interrupt your child while they are talking with someone or when they are in the middle of play or projects. If you must do so, start with "excuse me."

Teach your child that interrupting is bad manners and why, and then role-play situations, such as you being on the phone or having a face-to-face conversation with a spouse or friend. Practice is a too-often-overlooked parenting tool!

Teach your child what she can do if she really *needs* your attention while you are in the middle of a conversation, such as tug on your shirt. Also teach her the difference between needing your attention for something important and wanting it for something more trivial.

Acknowledge your child by putting a hand on her shoulder or winking at her, but unless you feel her interruption to be important, let her know you will be not be answering her until you are finished. Let her know your signs of acknowledgment (winking, shoulder touching) beforehand so that you don't have to interrupt your conversation to tell her this.

If you really need to finish a conversation and your child is too excited to wait, tell your listener "I will be just a few seconds" and then give your child your full attention and say "I really want to hear what you have to say. As soon as I am finished, I'll come to you." It does just take a few seconds, and if you consistently follow through, your child will learn its OK to wait until you're done with your conversation.

Be sure to keep your expectations realistic. Four year olds can wait longer than 2 year olds. Six year olds may only need reminders when they're very excited.

Scenario

You are on an important phone call. You have already explained to your child about interrupting, practiced it, and taught her how to get your attention. However, she is 4, and she's not perfect. So, during your call, she runs in and says, "Mom! How much longer are you going to be? I'm thirsty!"

Behind the behavior: Immature executive function. Teaching is necessary, but it takes time for little ones to master control over their impulses. She is not deliberately disobeying, she's just not able exercise restraint consistently yet.

ACTION: Give her your predetermined sign. Put your hand on her shoulder, wink at her, or hold up your index finger and smile. This will remind her of what you have practiced. If she gets louder or persists, kindly ask the other person to hold on for a minute, get down on eye level, explain that you are on the phone and cannot be interrupted right now, but that you will give her your full attention when you are off the phone. When

your call is over, practice again, and tell her
you're doing so to help her learn not to interrupt
again.

SUMMARY:

These small annoying behaviors do not last
forever. Guide her through them but realize
these are passing phases that will end with time
and maturity. Take a deep breath, remind
yourself of how fleeting childhood is, and try not
to take these smallies too seriously.

BACK TALK

Back talk is frequently an issue for parents, especially with older children, but the way you understand and handle it when it begins in early childhood will set the stage for whether or not you will have a problem with back talk later. All children will occasionally challenge their parents, but by having that connected relationship, you greatly reduce your chances of this becoming a problem behavior.

It is important to recognize that, in early childhood, children are just learning to assert themselves and separate from their parents. Therefore, what may be considered back talk can be re-framed in a more positive light of noticing our child's need for autonomy and respecting that need while teaching him appropriate and respectful ways to communicate their needs.

There are also indications that children who regularly practice debating (that's the positive version of talking back) are less susceptible to peer pressure. Let's look at a couple of scenarios to see how back talk should be addressed.

Scenario #1:

You have just asked your 2 year old to take his plate to the sink. He says, "No!"

Behind the Behavior: Confusion. He thinks "no" is a valid answer to the question. In many cultures, demands are 'softened' by wording them as questions. Small children (and even some older ones) think in literal terms, and when they hear, "Will you take your plate to the sink?" they interpret it to mean they have a choice.

ACTION: When actions are non-negotiable, word

them as statements, not questions. "Jack, I need for you to take your plate to the sink." If you *ask* for compliance, be willing to accept "no" as an answer. Because it's hard to change the way you speak, those times you asked instead of stating, admit your mistake and restate appropriately. "Jack, I know I asked if you would bring your plate to the sink, but I misspoke. I need for you to bring your plate to the sink before I finish loading the dishwasher."

If you find yourself giving orders all the time, start asking yourself if compliance really is necessary. A 2 year old not bringing his dinner dishes in does not mean he will grow up to be a slob with petrified pizza boxes under his couch when you come to visit. Don't compromise on your values, though. Neatness may be highly important for you. If so, find some other area where you can let go of the control. Nobody likes being ordered around all day and you will find compliance increasing when demands are lessened.

Scenario #2:

It's time for school, and your older child is sick and staying home from school, but you still need to get your 6 year old to class. Seeing that his sibling gets to stay home, he argues with you. "It's not fair that she doesn't have to go to school and I do!! I'm staying home, too!"

Behind the behavior: Jealousy. He wants to stay home like his sister. Life is very much about fairness with siblings, and any inequalities will be highlighted and remembered forever (so it seems).

ACTION: Set limits with empathy. With 2 or more kids and 1 or more adults in the family, it's not reasonable for everyone to stay home when one gets sick. "I know you don't want to go to school and would have a lot of fun staying home today. It's OK to be sad about it." Allow him to grieve before trying to get your message across. When you have competing messages, no one gets heard. Stick to the limit until he's calmed down. Then you can explain reasoning and offer up something else to think about. "Mary is sick and won't be having a great time, and I'll be busy taking care of her, so it probably wouldn't be a lot of fun anyway. I think you guys were going to talk about polar bears today. What's your favorite thing about them?"

Scenario #3:

You say something your daughter doesn't like

and she responds with, "You're stupid and I hate you!"

Behind the behavior: Hyperbole. Your child is upset and doesn't know how to express herself. She doesn't think you're stupid, she doesn't hate you, and she probably doesn't fully grasp the impact of what she is saying. When children feel safe with us, they let out emotions they're not comfortable expressing elsewhere. This means parents usually get to see a child's worst behavior.

ACTION: This is not about you, so replace "I hate you" with "I'm so upset I'm lashing out" in your mind. All feelings are OK, but not all behaviors are. Let your child hear that you understand she is upset but she needs to find another way to express it. It's important to keep this age appropriate though. For a 2 year old who says, "I don't love you anymore" you might say, "You're very mad at me. It's OK to be mad, but it makes me sad to hear you say you don't love me." It probably won't have any immediate effect on behavior, but over time, she'll learn how to identify those feelings and express them appropriately.

For school age children, you might say "It's OK to be upset, but it's not OK to talk to me like that. I understand that you're frustrated and would like for you to try to tell me more about how you're feeling in a way that doesn't attack me."

SUMMARY:

There are 2 keys to handling back talk in early childhood. The first key is understanding. If you can hear behind the "no" to what is really motivating your child, you take the personalization out of it. When it doesn't feel personal, it won't trigger feelings of anger and disrespect in you, and you'll be able to assess with a calm and rational mind what is motivating your child's action. The second key is empathy. It is important to validate your child's feelings so that he feels heard and understood. When he knows that you listen and care about what he feels and wants, the power struggle will dissipate much quicker than if you just assert your authority, which just invites a push-back response.

It is helpful to give your children as much control over their lives as is appropriate for their age, offer lots of acceptable choices throughout the day, and arrange their environment so they can help themselves as much as possible (i.e., having a low drawer with their cups and plates or having their snacks within reach so they can get it themselves).

Lastly, don't back talk back. It takes 2 people to have a power struggle. When you enforce your limits, do so with kindness and empathy, making sure your child feels heard and knows that you understand her point of view. By respecting her feelings, you're continuing to build on that bond, even if she doesn't get her way. As the years pass, she will forget the time she didn't get to skip school or go to a movie with her friends, but she will always remember how you made her feel and the relationship that you cultivated in early childhood.

LYING

Lying is actually a normal part of development. Punishment, or threat of punishment, only turns kids into better and more frequent liars.
Young children want to please their parents, so their "lie" is usually an attempt to make you happy or to try and please you. In this situation, it is best to stress the value of honesty rather than focus on the lie. Tell your child that the truth makes you happy. If there is no threat of punishment, and he knows telling the truth will make you happy, this challenges his original thought that hearing good news — not the truth — is what will please you. This type of "lie" in early childhood – told to please the parent – is a wish-fulfillment lie[13] whereby the child says something in hopes that saying it will make it true. At this stage, children often confuse a wish

with reality. Wish-fulfillment is very common in children up to age 7.

True lying, the purposefully deceitful kind, is actually a developmental milestone that isn't reached until around 7. A child who is going to deceitfully lie must recognize the truth, intellectually conceive of an alternate reality, and be able to convincingly sell that new reality to someone else. Therefore, deceitful lying demands both advanced cognitive development and social skills that toddlers and preschoolers simply do not possess.

So, how do we keep wish-fulfillment lies from becoming pathological?

Scenario #1:

Your 3 year old often forgets to wash her hands

after using the restroom. When she comes out, you ask if she's washed her hands, and she says she has, but you see her hands are dry.

Behind the behavior: She wants you to be pleased with her. It's difficult for a 3 year old to be consistent with any behavior and she probably forgot until you asked, but she does know now that you wanted her to wash her hands.

ACTION: Without shaming her, let her know that you know the truth. "Honey, I know that you wish you had washed your hands, but I see they are dry. Go back and wash your hands, please." This acknowledges her wish while separating it from reality.

Scenario #2:

Your 6 year old got into trouble at school for talking in class. His teacher already spoke to you about it. When you pick him up, you ask him if anything happened at school today. He tells you "nothing." Trying to get the truth out of him, you say, "Did you get into trouble at school today?" He says, "No."

Behind the behavior: Fear. He may fear punishment or disappointing you.

ACTION: If you know the answer to a question and it's likely to produce a lie, don't set him up. It is best to be forthright in these situations. Instead of asking him about it, be honest yourself. "I spoke with your teacher today and she tells me you lost recess for being disruptive in class." You can then work on problem-solving with your child to find solutions for not getting into trouble at school again.

SUMMARY:

When children feel unconditionally loved, and the threat of punishment is removed, lying will not become a pathological problem. There will be no need for the child to lie. It is important to model honesty and set a good example. Share with your children times it was difficult for you to tell the truth but you decided it was important to do so to retain your self-respect. Avoid telling them that "the park is closed" to avoid taking them and other little white lies because children catch on to them pretty quickly.

Help children to understand that mistakes are an opportunity to learn. Don't shame them or they may believe they are bad and feel the need to cover up their mistakes. Focus on solutions instead of blame. Rather than saying, "Did you clean your room?" when you know she didn't, say, "What can you do to ensure your chores get completed?"

Acknowledge honesty. "Thank you for telling the truth. I know that was difficult."

Don't overreact and call your child a liar. That is a label you never want to stick him with. **Remember that who your child is today is not who he will be forever.** He is growing and learning, and with your loving guidance, he will learn from his mistakes.

CHORES/RESPONSIBILITIES

I believe that chores are good for children. Chores help kids to feel competent, establish helpful habits, and teach real-world skills. The word *chores* is used to encompass all that goes into running a household, but since the very word is somewhat negative, when talking to your children, refer to the specific task at hand. How do we get children to do their chores without whining and complaining and without us having to nag at them to complete their chores? We do that by making it a fun, positive experience.

Children have different priorities than we do, so to expect them to want to jump up from playing and help us sweep is unreasonable. Many parents resort to bribes/rewards or consequences to get children to do their chores, but those tactics aren't necessary or helpful in the long run. Remember, we want our kids to be intrinsically motivated, and we want cooperation from a place of love and respect.

By practicing positive parenting, you already have an advantage because of the relationship you have developed with your child. Connection invites cooperation. Modeling is important with chores (as it is with everything we teach). If we grumble when we do our chores, we can expect our kids to do the same; however, if we approach our own chores with a positive attitude and express how good it feels once it is accomplished, our children can learn to adopt that attitude as well. Set age-appropriate tasks for your little ones, and give them adequate teaching before expecting them to complete the task on their own. Make chores as fun as possible by making games or beating timers. Most importantly, the mindset surrounding chores should be one of cooperation and togetherness, not of power struggles and forced drudgery. *The reason behind the behavior is obvious – it's not much fun – so we won't list that for each scenario.*

Scenario #1:

You have given your 2 year old the task of picking up her toys. It's now clean-up time.

ACTION: Little children usually love songs and dancing. Make up a short and cute clean-up song or put on some music. Not only will it help make it more fun, but she will begin to associate the song or music with clean-up time. If your child doesn't like songs/music, maybe beating the timer would be more fun. Go with your child's personality here, but for the sake of simplicity,

I'm just going to use the song for this scenario. Start singing the song, being silly, and dancing around while you pick up the toys. Invite her to join in. She will likely want in on the fun. If she resists, just continue to model the behavior. Be careful not to make it a power struggle, which might set the stage for chore struggles in the future. She's just 2, so resisting to clean up toys doesn't mean she'll never clean her room as a teenager. She'll learn.

Scenario #2:

Sweeping is the chosen task for your 3 year old. (It is a good idea to let them choose from 2 or 3 chores which one they'd prefer.)

ACTION: To make it a game, you can block out a square on the floor with painter's tape and have him try to sweep everything into that square. At this young age, we're still working on teaching the idea of responsibility and making it more appealing than we are on him doing a great job at all by himself, which is probably not going to happen for several more years. If he occasionally resists, I wouldn't consider it a big deal, but if he consistently doesn't want to do his chore, you may want to consider letting him choose a different chore or changing up your strategy.

Scenario #3

Six year old David's room is often a mess. He constantly has laundry on the floor, books strewn about, and an unmade bed. You've told him dozens of times to keep his room clean and have even threatened to take away his video games as a consequence, but this continues to be a problem.

ACTION: Chronic problems require problem-solving, not consequences. If you're not already having regular family meetings, now is a good time to start. During family meetings, address any problems or concerns each family member is having and work on solutions everyone can agree on. Include some positive conversation in your family meetings as well, recognizing accomplishments and planning vacations or weekend trips. You don't want "family meeting" to have a negative connotation.

Call a meeting and ask David, "How can we help you be successful in keeping your room clean?" Get ideas from each member and map out a plan for David's success. One scenario may be that a special time is set aside each week where everyone cleans their respective rooms. Occasionally, each person could go check on the others' progress and offer encouragement, such as "you did it!" or "you're almost done!" After the cleanup, everyone can meet at the table for some quality family time.

SUMMARY:

I have found visual charts to be helpful. These charts are not associated with rewards but serve purely as a visual reminder.

If you'll remain positive and develop the team-player attitude in your home, your child will learn to do chores without the power struggle many parents face in this regard. Allow for some off days and allow your children to negotiate when it comes to which chores and at what time they are done. Keep it fun, keep it positive, and keep it a priority because your child will benefit from responsibility.

SIBLING RIVALRY

You imagine they will be best friends, walking hand in hand, playing together every day, but then you get a big dose of reality when your children fight with each other. You may have found yourself playing referee on a daily basis, but the good news is that you can teach them how to manage their relationship themselves by stepping out of the referee role and becoming what Genevieve Simperingham calls an "empathetic mediator" in her article, The Peaceful Parenting Approach to Kids' Conflicts (see www.peaceful-parent.com).[14] An empathetic mediator supports each person through the conflict rather than serving as a referee aimed at deciding who's right and who's wrong. When you teach your children problem-solving skills, you'll soon find they can come up with their own solutions to their disputes. This will prove to be a much more valuable lesson than if you were to assign consequences and solutions.

How do you teach children problem-solving skills? You start by being that empathetic mediator when your children have a disagreement. Listen to each child, empathizing with their upset and understanding their point of view. Refrain from making a judgment and delivering your verdict, but instead walk through the process of problem-solving with them. Here's what it looks like in action.

Scenario #1:

Sally (5) is playing with her teddy bear. Her sister, Emma (3), grabs the teddy bear from Sally. Sally tries to grab it back and they end up in a tug of war, both yelling at each other to "stop it!"

Behind the behavior: Competition. Both children want the same thing, but they don't know how to negotiate. Many toys become desirable just because someone else has it. Some kids also use snatching as a way to initiate play.

ACTION: State what you see happening. "You both want to play with the teddy bear. How can we solve this?" Wait for their suggestions at this point, if they come. If not, throw some out there. "One of you could pick a different toy to play with, or you can take turns with the teddy bear. Which sounds best to you?" Realize this is not likely to go smoothly at first, but you're teaching a valuable lesson here. Validate each child's feelings. If Sally says, "Mom! I was playing with it and she stole it!" then you might say, "I understand that you're frustrated she took your toy. I will talk to her about snatching later."

Emma chimes in "Not yours! It's mine!" so you say, "You think it's your bear and didn't want Sally to have it." Often feeling heard and validated dissipates the anger. Once you help them reach a solution, show them how to carry it through. If they decided to take turns with it, they may need your help if they don't understand the concept that well yet. Later, when Emma is calm, talk to her about the importance of being respectful to her sister, and how snatching is not respectful but instead she should use her words to ask for the teddy bear, then practice doing that with her.

Scenario #2:

Michael (6) and Nelly (5) are picking on each other. From the kitchen, you hear Katie call Michael a "stupid face" and Michael retaliates with a "smelly Nelly."

Behind the behavior: Jealousy? Aggravation? It just depends on what incited the argument, and you'll have to do some investigating to find out what it was.

ACTION: "I hear name-calling. That is against our family rules. What is going on?" You've restated your limit of no name-calling. Now to find out what is happening. Katie: "Michael knocked over my block tower! He's so stupid!" You: "You're angry that he knocked over your blocks, but name calling isn't allowed." Michael: "I didn't mean to knock it over! It was an accident!" You: "Okay, so you accidentally knocked over your sister's block tower. She got upset and called you a name. That hurt your feelings, so you called her a name. What could have been done differently?" If they don't come up with ideas, offer that Michael could have made it clear that it was an accident and offered to help build it back and that Nelly could have stated she was disappointed about her tower without the name-calling. Reiterate to both them that name-calling is disrespectful and against family rules. If they do not come to peace, you may need to tell them to separate for the time being and follow through with making sure they are separated or, if the name-calling continues, a time-in (staying with your child and helping him to calm down rather than forcing isolation) in a calm down corner may be appropriate to enforce your limit.

Each child should feel safe and comfortable in his or her own home. Allowing one child to be constantly bullied or taunted by the other one isn't fair to that child. Set appropriate boundaries that respect each individual in the home and that create an atmosphere of acceptance and love, not rivalry and conflict. When conflicts arise, be the empathetic mediator and help them to learn to problem-solve on their own. This may take some time, but it is a worthwhile investment for your sanity and peace.

Even if you have very young children, such as a 2 year old and a 10 month old, and verbal skills are very limited, you can still talk through this process while you mediate the dispute.

SUMMARY:

Peaceful parenting is about having peaceful homes and peaceful relationships. Conflicts will always arise, and that is perfectly normal, but by setting boundaries around respect and teaching problem-solving skills, we can teach our kids how to find solutions, repair relationships, and come back to peace.

PEER INFLUENCE

Inevitably, when your child is around other children at daycare, playgroups, or school, her peers will have an influence on her. What do you do when your child picks up negative behavior from her peers? The good news here again is that the strong bond you have built through positive parenting is going to be your ally in defense against bad influences. It is wise, however, to realize that all significant persons in your child's life - relatives, teachers, religious leaders, and friends - all affect her values and self-concept, and it is up to you to screen out those who drag her down and to encourage those who build her up. If your connection is strong, your influence will ultimately overcome the peer's influence. Of course, she will try out some of the behaviors she has learned, but with your guidance, she will know what her limits are and will stay within those boundaries. As she grows, this will help her set limits for herself and resist negative peer influences in the future.

Scenario #1:

You can't believe your ears when you hear your sweet 3 year old use profanity. When you ask her where she heard that word, she tells you a kid at daycare said it.

Behind the behavior: Imitation. Children learn from what is modeled and will try out novel experiences. Chances are there was a reaction when the other child said it and yours wants to see if the same is true when she says it.

ACTION: State your limit, "I don't like that word. Please don't say that again." Be mindful not to overreact as this may cause her to repeat it just to get your reaction or attention. If she repeats it immediately, ignore it and focus her attention on something else. It is likely she will forget all about the word. The bigger the issue you make of it, the more likely she will remember it. *What you focus on, you get more of.*

Scenario #2:

You don't allow your 6 year old to play violent video games, but apparently his best friend does play them, because your son has started pretend fighting and shooting things. When asked where he learned about fighting and guns, he tells you he plays this way with his friend at school. During one of his pretend fighting episodes, he accidentally makes contact with his brother's stomach. Plus, he wants you to buy him the game.

Behind the behavior: Imprinting. Until about age 9, a child's brain does very little filtering and things that are experienced are essentially accepted without question. Video games and TV violence desensitizes people and makes it more likely they will act aggressively at other times. Executive function, which allows someone to delay gratification for greater rewards, plan ahead, and set long term goals, takes two and a half decades to mature. Some people never learn to delay gratification. Your son's friend is offering something that will be very difficult for him to resist.

ACTION: Your older son is having a negative impact on his brother and you, so you need to be assertive with your needs. Many times people don't realize the impact their actions are having on someone and will willingly change them when it's brought to their attention in a way that doesn't make them defensive. The approach most likely to get your message heard consists of a factual description of the behavior, the tangible effect it has on you, and your feelings about it.

An example might be, "I'm worried (feeling) that your brother or someone else might get seriously hurt (tangible effect) when you imitate violent games at home (behavior)." Be on the lookout for hidden judgments or blaming statements in the behavior part, such as "when you are so violent" or "if you keep playing those horrible games."

If this is not enough to improve the situation, a negotiated contract with expected behaviors may help. In order to have your child accept the contract, they do have to feel a sense of ownership by being involved in the process.

Laying down the law only invites resistance and children will intuitively pick up any attempts at manipulation. Focus on your needs, not a solution you've already devised. It can be challenging to isolate your needs from a solution in the beginning. Not playing video games is a solution. Ensuring a safe environment is a need.

Help your child focus on his needs. Playing video games is a solution. Fitting in is a need. Then brainstorm some ideas about how you can both get your needs met. Children as young as 2 or 3 can propose solutions, but you'll get better results with older children and practice.

If a solution doesn't work for both of you, it doesn't work. Keep trying! When you have something that appears workable, agree to try it out for a period of time and then come back to evaluate its effectiveness. You'll need to know what constitutes success and what the time frame is when you'll revisit the contract. If it's working, congratulations! If it's not, brainstorm again.

As tempting as it is to just forbid contact, this almost always doesn't work. You won't be able to keep them apart at school and you may inadvertently push them closer by making the relationship more enticing because it isn't allowed. Your child may no longer want to be friends with someone but be unsure how to 'get out of it' gracefully. The key is really listening to what is going on with him.

SUMMARY:

The older a child gets, the less control of her environment we have. As outside influences grow, our ability to guide our children relies more and more on our connection with them not our power over them. By involving our children in the problem-solving process early on, when relative risks are low, we enable them to tackle bigger issues later on when we're not there to make decisions for them. It's also more likely they will seek our advice for problems we're not aware of if we aim to provide them tools instead of fixes.

When it comes to relationships that don't directly involve you, try to trust your child to handle it. He will make some mistakes, without a doubt, but they are his mistakes and he needs to feel safe in making them. He may also get something out of the relationship that you wouldn't, and that's OK, too. Don't be afraid to be assertive, though, if the relationship negatively affects you in a concrete way - everyone in the family counts.

MEALTIMES

Whether you have a picky eater or a food thrower, mealtimes can sometimes be challenging with young children. We want to establish healthy eating habits in our children, so frustration builds when they refuse to eat their vegetables or want to live on cookies and chips. The tricky part is, of course, that we can't *make* them eat. All we can do is offer healthy options. But mealtime struggles go beyond the picky eater to refusing to sit in the high chair, booster, or seat, throwing food, etc.

To make mealtimes more enjoyable for everyone, I think there are 2 keys. One is to keep in mind what is age-appropriate when you consider your expectations. A toddler can't be expected to sit still at the dinner table for 30 minutes. The second key is flexibility. Set the boundaries you feel are most important and stick to them, but also be flexible where you can afford to be.

Let's take a look at a few scenarios that can make mealtimes a dreaded time of day and what you can do to bring back the peace.

Scenario #1:

While you have diligently tried to instill healthy eating habits, your toddler simply refuses anything green, anything squishy, and anything round.

Behind the behavior: Like all of us, sometimes toddlers just aren't in the mood for certain foods. Have you ever been in the hospital and had no say over what your meals were going to be, and you just had to hope there was something on the menu you liked? That's probably how a toddler feels every day.

ACTION: If you don't want your toddler to eat junk food, don't buy junk food. If you have to have it in the house, put it out of sight. Make sure to offer at least one thing at each meal that you know your child likes. Continue offering healthy options as sides, even if he's refused them before. Toddlers' tastes change frequently. What was great yesterday may be gross today, and vice versa. Try as best you can to avoid food power struggles. Offer healthy options consistently, but realize that ultimately it is up to your child what he likes and what he eats. If there are only mostly nutritious foods in the house, there will, of course, be less of a problem.

Scenario #2:

Your 20 month old is testing gravity...with her pasta. She hurls it off the high chair and giggles hysterically. You're not finding it funny.

Behind the behavior: She's simply discovering. Food has interesting properties, too, and children learn by manipulating objects. She doesn't have any concept of wasting food or creating more work for you - it's just fun.

ACTION: "Hey silly girl, food stays in your plate. If you throw it, you must not be hungry. Are you hungry?" If she throws it again, remove the plate and say, "Food stays in the plate, sweetie. I guess you're not hungry right now. If you want to throw, let's go throw a ball! We'll come back to your food in a little bit." Give her 15 or 20 minutes and try again. Throwing the food will lose its appeal soon enough. If she's hungry, she will eat it.

Scenario #3:

Your 3 year old won't stay at the table for more than 5 minutes. He wants to stand in his chair or run off.

Behind the behavior: Life's too short to waste it *just* eating! Toddlers are typically not able to sit still through an entire meal. Some will have more patience than others, but you can generally count on less than 10 minutes at age 3.

ACTION: Encourage sitting at the table, but don't force it. Bottoms in the chair, for safety's sake, if he's going to be at the table. The stress it adds to dinnertime isn't worth the energy spent trying to corral an active toddler. If you regularly model sitting down for meals, eventually he will spend more and more time in his seat until he's able to make it the whole meal.

I'm against restraining a child's movement for our convenience. As Maria Montessori says, "Only through freedom and environmental experience is it practically possible for human development to occur."[15] Children as young as a year old can learn to sit independently on small chairs. Highchairs may keep him at the table for now, but they don't teach him how to regulate himself so that he can stay there willingly.

Make his spot toddler-friendly with easy access to come and go on his own. A small table and chair next to the family table allows him to participate but doesn't require any help to get down (or the risk of toppling a chair over and getting hurt).

Institute a *no toys* policy at the table. He's more likely to want to join you if you're talking to each other and not texting. This also allows you to say, "It's dinnertime, toys stay put up" when he wants to create with play doh.

The more positive associations your child has around mealtimes, the less likely he is to develop unhealthy habits.

Scenario #4:

Your 6 year old son almost always protests whatever you have made for dinner and asks for something else.

Behind the behavior: Autonomy. Even at 6, your son's world is pretty small. Meals can be a big part of it to him and if he has no say, it may leave him feeling a little out of control.

ACTION: I have heard many parents state they aren't short order cooks (and this is certainly true) and some experts advise to make them eat what you have fixed or go hungry. It is my opinion that, while we aren't short order cooks, it is our job to meet the needs of our children, and allowing them to go hungry is not meeting their need for nutritious meals. There are a couple of options. The first option is to let your child help you plan the menu. This way, you know there is something on there that he will enjoy. The second option is to teach young children how to make themselves basic small meals, such as a sandwich. Tell him he is free to make himself a sandwich if he doesn't like what is on the table. A third option which is good for young children is to have an accessible snack bin in your refrigerator or a bowl on the counter filled with pre-bagged items, such as apples, yogurt, graham crackers, bananas, cheese and crackers, etc. This way, you don't have to fix a separate meal, but they have nutritious options at their fingertips.

SUMMARY:

Forcing children to eat when they're not hungry or eat foods they hate may predispose them to eating disorders later. Allowing young children to go hungry is ignoring their need for food. However, that doesn't mean we have to give into their demand for pizza every night. In fact, giving in to constant demands for unhealthy foods also puts them at risk for obesity and health issues. It is our responsibility to offer a variety of nutritious foods and to ensure that they eat enough food for health and growth. Stocking your refrigerator with nutritious options and having the courtesy to put at least one thing on your menu you know your child likes will cut down on most food power struggles.

Learning to sit through an entire meal is a developmental milestone. Your child will get there! Until then, be flexible, and remember that this too shall pass!

POTTY LEARNING

After a couple of years of toting around heavy diaper bags and changing diapers on those flimsy changing tables in public, not to mention the high cost of diapering if you're using disposables, it's no wonder that many of us are in a hurry to get our kids potty trained. There is a vast age range in which children can show signs of readiness, from before the age of 2 to well past 3 or even 4.

Signs of readiness include:

• Ability to express and understand words such as "wet," "dry," "potty," and "go."

• Having dry periods of at least 3 to 4 hours or is dry after a nap. This shows signs that the bladder muscles are developed enough to hold urine.

- Showing interest in the potty or other people's bathroom habits.
- Showing imitative behavior.
- Dislikes the feeling of a wet or soiled diaper.
- Ability to pull pants up and down.

Forcing a child to train too early is associated with a whole host of issues. On the other hand, occasionally children do need a positive nudge in the direction of potty learning, particularly if they are showing signs of readiness but are still somewhat hesitant to give up diapers. Following your child's cues is important in this process. All babies get out of diapers eventually, and the myth that the longer you allow them to wear diapers, the harder they will be to train, is false.

Let's look at how a positive parent handles a couple of potty training scenarios.

Scenario #1:

Your 2-1/2 year old daughter shows signs that she is ready to potty train. You let her pick out a potty seat, buy a potty doll and book, and even let her choose her underwear. The problem is that she gets hysterical when you try to sit her on the potty. All of your attempts to calm her are futile; she just seems really against the potty.

Behind the behavior: Fear or not being emotionally ready. It has been said that you cannot force a child to eat, sleep, or eliminate. She may feel too pressured by being placed on the seat or the whole idea may just be too much at the time.

ACTION: Just because she may be showing some of the typical physical signs doesn't mean she is cognitively or emotionally ready to train yet. It is common for a child to show some hesitation, but crying, screaming, and persistent refusal indicates that she is just not ready yet. Indicate that it's not a big deal and that she can do as much as she's ready for, even if it's sitting on the potty fully clothed for a while. Give her some more time and try again when she is a little older.

Scenario #2

Your son just turned 4. He's been peeing in the potty for more than 4 months now, but he still has accidents with soiling his underwear.

Behind the behavior: There could a medical issue, such as constipation which causes fear of painful bowel movements which in turn causes him to hold it until it begins to leak out. He could also have a fear of the potty (falling in) or fear of having a bowel movement on the potty.

ACTION: Make sure he gets enough fiber and try to keep his stools soft and regular. At this point, you don't want to go back to diapers since he's been out of them now for several months; this would just cause more confusion. Set regular intervals where you take him to sit on the potty, perhaps every hour or so. Let him choose whether he wants to use a small potty or a potty seat on the big potty. There are several children's books available about this issue as well that may be helpful to your child. Avoid punishing, threatening, or shaming as this will only make matters worse. Just remember that this too shall pass. No pun intended.

SUMMARY:

Potty learning is different for every child. Some get it immediately, and for others, it takes a long time. Some initiate it themselves; others may need a gentle nudge. Watch for signs of readiness and allow your child to have some control over the whole process, such as picking out a potty seat, underwear, and so forth. If your child adamantly refuses, give it more time. If she is hesitant but willing, give her a gentle nudge. If he initiates potty learning himself, count your lucky stars! Either way, keep the process positive, avoiding punishments, guilt, shame, or threats. Have fun with it, doing dances or popping balloons for each time she uses the potty. It may seem like the process is never going to end, but I promise that one day you'll look back on those diaper days fondly and wish she was back in them, right under your feet again.

NIGHT TIMES

From bedtime battles to multiple night wakings, every parent will struggle with some sort of night time issue at one time or another. There are entire books dedicated to helping children get in bed and sleep soundly, and covering the many sleep and bedtime-related issues is beyond the scope of this book, but we do want to show you what Positive Parenting in Action looks like during some of the most common issues that arise when the sun goes down.

Scenario #1:

Your 12 month old still wakes multiple times through the night. Shouldn't he be sleeping through the night by now? Your friend has suggested you sleep train him, claiming it worked like a charm for her 8 month old.

Behind the behavior: Physiology. Sleeping through the night is a myth. Young children have shorter cycles of light and deep sleep, and they are physiologically programmed to wake up more often than adults.[16] If your child is sleeping alone, he may be experiencing separation anxiety when he finds himself awake and alone. Young children also have trouble sorting dreams from reality and may wake disoriented or frightened. Children need parents to be just as available during the night as they are during the day.

ACTION: Never leave a young child to cry unattended. Not only does it sever trust and damage your relationship, but the rise in cortisol levels of a child left to cry kills brain cells.[17] Children left to cry themselves to sleep are prone to suffer from anxiety[18], panic attacks, and other mental disorders later in life. A child sleep-trained through the cry-it-out method does not sleep through the night **but rather has learned that no one will come to help when he calls.**

Meet the needs of your child through the night just as you do through the day. There are things you can do to facilitate a more restful night, such as having a consistent routine, a comfortable, dark room, white noise or comforting sounds, and experimenting with different sleeping arrangements, *but the fact is that young children need to be parented back to sleep*. Use these bleary-eyed, quiet moments to savor this fleeting time of childhood. It is exhausting, but one day you'll back fondly on those nights you spent rubbing his back or rocking him to sleep.

Scenario #2

Your 3 year old falls asleep in his bed but always

comes to your bed sometime in the middle of night. Your family prefers to not co-sleep, and you want him to stay in his own bed all night.

Behind the behavior: It is possible that he is experiencing separation anxiety or nighttime fears. Or perhaps he just misses you and wants to be close.

ACTION: Ensure that he is getting enough of your undivided attention and nurturing touch during the day. Take him back to his bed and lie down with him or sit near him until he is asleep again, or very drowsy. You can stick to your limit while still meeting his needs. This may take a lot of patience and repetition on your part, but your relationship will remain intact and his trust in you will not waiver.

Scenario #3:

It is bedtime for your 5 year old daughter. When you ask her to get ready for bed, she says, "Why do I have to go to bed? I'm not tired! I don't want to go to bed yet!"

Behind the behavior: Autonomy. She wants to make decisions for herself. Many times the bedtime routine evolves into a to-do list that the parents check off before they get some couple time (or alone time). Children feel rushed and unheard and balk, leading to bedtime battles. If it's been particularly hectic, she may need some extra attention, too. It is also possible that her bedtime is too early or too late. If it is too early, she won't be tired enough for sleep. If it is too late, she may be overly tired and have a second wind. There could be many other reasons for her procrastination as well; fear of the dark,

separation anxiety, nightmares, etc.

ACTION: Create a routine if you don't already

have one. It helps them know what's coming so

bedtime isn't a surprise. Then make sure you

plan plenty of time for it. An hour or more is

most likely necessary. It takes some time to wind

down, and rushing through the routine makes

everyone feel … rushed. Many parents find it

helpful to match pictures of the routine chart

with pictures of analog clocks (the ones with

hands) so that it becomes the bad guy instead of

the parent. "The chart says we read books until

the big hand is on the 3, then lights out. It's on

the 3, so lights out!"

Adjusting bedtime, providing a night light, or

lying down with her may help, depending on the

reason behind the behavior. If she is frightened, don't downplay her fears. They're real to her. Try to keep everything in your routine relaxing. A bath, reading, massage, and songs will help slow things down and let your child get sleepy. TV, video games, or chasing each other through the house will make it more difficult to transition to sleep. Elizabeth Pantley offers more ideas in her *No Cry Sleep Solution* book.

Also consider that your child may just need some more time reconnecting with you after a long absence or hard day. If your evenings are typical, there's not a lot of down time spent just hanging out and she's reluctant to let go of you once she has your undivided attention. Try spending 10-15 minutes focused solely on her when you both meet after the day and limit distractions during your bedtime routine. Staying until she falls asleep may help.

Scenario #4:

Lindsay is 3 and has always been a consistent napper, until now. Suddenly she is refusing her afternoon nap. By 5 pm., she starts to get cranky.

Behind the behavior: She may be transitioning out of the need for a nap, but if she is cranky in the evening, she will likely still benefit from at least some resting time.

ACTION: While you can't force a resistant napper to sleep, you can create an environment that is inviting for sleep or rest. Having a consistent routine around nap time will help, such as lunch, story, and then nap. Make sure the room is comfortable and dim or dark. She may be tired but not sleepy, and trying to force her to nap may cause her to view her bed as a punishment place, which is definitely something you don't want to have happen. A few ideas to try are a *nap nook* (a special place elsewhere that she helps to create, such as a pile of blankets in the corner or a tent made of sheets. You can also try a new routine of going for a stroll or car ride, which often puts children to sleep, or carving out special quiet time where there is no pressure to fall asleep but quiet activities and rest are encouraged. Around age 3, some children are ready to give up their naps and move to an earlier bedtime.

SUMMARY:

Sleeping, like eating and pottying, is something you can't force upon a child. These are areas where they have complete control, and our job as parents is to facilitate healthy habits to the best of our ability. Ensuring that your child gets enough exercise and sunshine during the day will help him to sleep better at night. Remaining responsive and compassionate during nighttime hours is important to the healthy development of your child, and to your relationship.

OUT AND ABOUT

Many parents feel forced/coerced/shamed into parenting differently under the gazing eyes of strangers or family. Even though you may practice positive parenting at home, when you are out and about, the peer pressure to follow more traditional guidelines can cause you to compromise your instincts, in turn compromising your relationship with your child. Of course, a strong, connected relationship will recover from such occasional breaks, but we still want to be mindful when we are parenting in public that our children are our first responsibility. Focusing on onlookers will undermine your ability to help your child, so it is best to block out their stares and judgments and stay true to your parenting style. At the end of the day, it is your child whom you are going home with, not the strangers at the store or the grandparents.

To minimize the chance for behavioral issues while you are out and about, it is important to be mindful of your children's needs. Ensure they are not hungry or overly tired. Explain to your child where you are going, what you will be doing, and what to expect, along with what you expect. If it is a first for your child, it is helpful to practice the scene beforehand so that your child has a firmer grasp on what is expected. Even if it is not a first, but you have had trouble before, such as at the grocery store, practicing is always a good idea.

If a meltdown happens in public, and it probably will at some point, stay present with your child, offer empathy, and stick to your limit, just as you do at home. Even though you may feel like everyone is judging what a terrible parent you are, the opposite is likely the case. They are probably sympathizing with you as most every parent has been in this situation. It is important to balance your child's needs and emotions with socially acceptable behavior, though, as her behavior does affect those who are around her.

Scenario #1:

You're at the library with your 16 month old son. He gets upset and throws himself onto the floor in a tantrum. Several people turn their eyes toward you and your child. (See the section on Tantrums).

Behind the behavior: Being overwhelmed. Toddlers can tire quickly when they're out and about. They may also get overstimulated or hungry or have the need to just be home in their familiar surroundings.

ACTION: Remember that empathy is the first course of action when dealing with heavy emotions. Showing empathy never spoils a child or teaches them to throw fits to get their way. Rather, it builds trust as they learn you are there for them through troubled times, helps build brain circuits so that they can better handle their emotions in the future, and meets their need to be understood and heard. If your child doesn't want physical comfort, or even verbal comfort, respect that and give him space, but let him know you are there if he needs you. One of the hardest things to do is to support your child through one of these moments in front of other people instead of shushing him or trying distraction or bribes, but you really are doing him a great service by being present and empathic during this time. Hopefully the onlookers will learn a thing or two about empathy. Our culture could certainly use more of it.

Scenario #2:

You're heading to the grocery store with 3 kids in tow. You are prepared with a list for each child to help with, an activity bag in your purse, and you've explained ahead of time where you are going and what you will be getting. Everything should go smoothly, right? You've made wonderful preparations, and that is really smart, but as we all know, sometimes you get thrown a curve ball.

It just so happens that your 4 year old is not interested in the list OR the activity bag. He is interested only in talking you into buying him a new Lego set, even though you clearly stated you wouldn't be buying toys this trip. When you restate your limit, he begins to stomp and whine.

Behind the behavior: Desire. Ownership and its transfer via symbolic wealth is a nebulous concept for many years. It can be a bit confusing to small children to walk into a store with rows and rows of fascinating things and only leave with a small, apparently random, assortment. Your child may be able to repeat back rules about paying for things, but he doesn't fully understand why he can't just have what he wants. Especially, when from his perspective, you pick up the things you want.

Younger children may believe that you can *just buy* anything they want or need, like rainbows. Before they're around 8, children may not understand being employed for an income and why that's necessary to buy things.

ACTION: Empathize. There's something he wants and he doesn't understand why you're keeping it from him. If you have a calm down travel bag handy, it may help to let him squeeze out his frustration with a stress ball or calm down with the *I Spy Jar* or *Calm Down Jar*. You can also try fantasizing with him. "Wow, that is a great toy. I bet you'd like to have every Lego ever made! What could you build if you had all the Legos ever made?" If you have the time, allow them to play with toys on the condition that they don't make them unsellable and that they put them back when you need to leave. They have probably seen you pick up something you're interested in and check it out. Maybe it's the nutrition label and not your idea of fun, but from their view, it's unfair you get to do it and they have to keep their hands to themselves.

Stick to your limit (if you don't want to guarantee a tantrum every time) but look for ways to involve him in the process. Maybe you ask him to pick out apples or find the biggest bag of flour or choose a dessert. If he's not tired, hungry, or overstimulated, and you've listened with empathy and offered alternatives, you may just have to let him be in a bad mood about it. All feelings are valid. "Sweetie, I know you're disappointed about not getting the Legos. We're going to finish shopping and you can join in when you're ready."

Scenario #3:

It's a beautiful day, and you've been at the park with your daughter for more than an hour. It's time to go, and you've given ample warning that this time was near. She ignores you or runs away from you when you try to get her to the car.

Behind the behavior: Her need to play! She's having fun and wants to keep playing. Ever tried to end a conversation with someone and ended up talking another half hour? Even with ample warning, some transitions are hard. She may really resist if it's been a long time since she's gotten out or if the next activity doesn't seem like much fun.

ACTION: Try a playful game. "Let's hop to the car like kangaroos" or "race you!" If she still stalls, just pick her up and carry her to the car. You can do this kindly and gently, empathizing that you understand she doesn't want to leave because she is having fun. "It was a lot of fun to climb and play today, and you're very sad it's over. It's time for us to leave and I can't let you run off." Again, the difference in positive parenting is the way in which we enforce our limits. While an authoritarian parent may be very upset and scold the child for "not minding," we follow through on our limits with understanding and a kind smile. When you remain kind and loving when you enforce your limits, the child accepts them more readily, and, very importantly, the attachment remains strong.

Scenario #4:

You are eating at a fairly nice restaurant (no play lands this time!) and your 3 year old keeps standing in the seat and talking loudly.

Behind the behavior: Boredom. Three year olds find eating relatively boring and the other people are interesting to watch. Especially when they make faces at loud noises.

ACTION: It's a good idea to have an activity bag made up and in your purse for such occasions, or something your child likes to do; perhaps a small coloring book or quiet toy. It's also good to practice these scenarios at home fairly often so she knows what to do when the time comes. However, if, despite your practice and goodie bags, she is still standing up and/or being loud, take her to the bathroom or outside for a time-in. Try to elicit her help. Explain that everyone is trying to enjoy a quiet meal and ask how she can help them. Walk through the problem-solving steps with her. "The people behind us are trying to enjoy their meal and they don't seem to like so much noise. What fun things could we do that are quiet?"

Offer her some choices and give her some room to move, if it's feasible. "Would you like to sit with me or Daddy?" "You may sit on your bottom in the chair, or stand next to me." When you think she is ready to go back to the table, tell her what is expected, and that she will be taken away from the table again if she is loud or disruptive. You may have to do this more than once, and people may be watching, but you're teaching her the value of your word and what is acceptable in public places. I know this doesn't make for a lovely, calm dinner for you, but if you're consistent, you can look forward to a lovely, calm dinner soon!

You may need to reset your expectations and visit family-friendly establishments until she's a bit older, or get a sitter.

SUMMARY:

Children have a right to be in public as much as anyone else, but they also have a responsibility to follow social conventions as much as is developmentally appropriate. Keeping them home does not teach them how to behave. Try to be prepared, stay flexible, and treat them with the same love, respect, and empathy that you do at home.

CONCLUSION

There is no One Right Way to parent. Each child and each parent is an individual with different thoughts, feelings, and desires. We believe that the positive parenting philosophy embodies the values we hope to pass on to our children and supports our instincts to be responsive, supportive, and influential. At the core is mutual respect, and so, regardless of the strategies you adopt or the words you use, ask yourself "how would I feel if that were done to me?"

We hope that you have found this book to be enlightening and helpful to your family. We wish you all the best on your parenting journey. Thanks for letting us be a part of it.

~ Rebecca & Laura

There is no single effort more radical in its

potential for saving the world than a

transformation in the way we raise our children.

– Marianne Williamson

REFERENCES:

1. Markham, Dr. Laura. N.p., n. d. 1 Jul 2013.
    <http://www.ahaparenting.com/_blog/Parenting_Blog/p
    ost/Are_You_Too_Strict_or_Too_Permissive/>.

2. McLeod, S. A. (2007). *Carl Rogers - Simply Psychology.*
    Retrieved from http://www.simplypsychology.org/carl-
    rogers.html

3. . N.p.. Web. 1 Jul 2013.
    <http://www.attachmentparenting.org/Infantsleepsafety
    />.

4. . N.p.. Web. 1 Jul 2013.
    <http://www.attachmentparenting.org/principles/princip
    les.php>.

5. Randy , W. n. page.
    <http://www.whitehutchinson.com/leisure/articles/76.sh
    tml>.

6. . N.p., 2008.
    <http://www.hhs.gov/opa/familylife/tech_assistance/etr
    aining/adolescent_brain/Development/prefrontal_cortex
    />.

7. Horowitz, S.. N.p.. Web. 1 Jul 2013.
   <http://www.umass.edu/fambiz/articles/values_culture/
   primal_leadership.html>.

8. Markham, Laura. N.p., n. d. 1 Jul 2013.

9. Government of New South Wales , . N.p.. Web. 1 Jul
   2013.
   <http://www.community.nsw.gov.au/docswr/_assets/ma
   in/documents/aggression_discussionpaper.pdf>.

10. Kohn, Alfie. *Beyond Discipline, From Compliance To
    Community*. 10th Anniversary. Alexandria, Virgina:
    Association for Supervision & Curriculum Developme,
    2006. Print.

11. Sears, William, and Martha Sears. *The Discipline Book*.
    NYC: Little, Brown and Co., 1995. Print.

12. Markham, D. L.. N.p.. Web. 1 Jul 2013.
    <http://www.ahaparenting.com/ages-
    stages/preschoolers/life-preschooler/pre-empt-whining>.

13. Ford, C. V. *Lies! lies!! lies!!*. First. Washington DC:
    American Psychiatric Press, Inc., 1996. Print.

14. Simperingham, Genevieve. N.p.. Web. 1 Jul 2013.
    <http://www.peaceful-
    parent.com/article_children's_conflicts_peaceful_parenti
    ng_approach.php>.

15. Montessori, M.. N.p.. Web. 1 Jul 2013.
    <http://www.dailymontessori.com/maria-montessori-quotes/>.

16. Roth, K.. N.p.. Web. 1 Jul 2013.
    <http://yoursleep.aasmnet.org/topic.aspx?id=59>.

17. Thomas, R.M., Hotsenpiller,G. & Peterson, D.A. (2007). Acute Psychosocial Stress Reduces Cell Survival in Adult Hippocampal Neurogenesis without Altering Proliferation. The Journal of Neuroscience, 27(11): 2734-2743.

18. Narvaez, D. n.d. n. page. <http://www.psychologytoday.com/blog/moral-landscapes/201112/recovering-cry-it-out-parenting-adult>.